D0444379

A People in Focus Book

Benazir Bhutto

FROM
PRISON
TO
PRIME
MINISTER

Libby Hughes

AN AUTHORS GUILD BACKINPRINT.COM EDITION

Benazir Bhutto:

From Prison to Prime Minister

All Rights Reserved © 1990, 2000 by Libby Hughes

No part of this book may be reproduced or transmitted in any form
or by any means, graphic, electronic, or mechanical, including photocopying,
recording, taping, or by any information storage or retrieval system,
without the permission in writing from the publisher.

AN AUTHORS GUILD BACKINPRINT.COM EDITION

Published by iUniverse, Inc.

For information address:
iUniverse, Inc.
5220 S. 16th St., Suite 200
Lincoln, NE 68512
www.iuniverse.com

Originally published by Dillon Press, Inc.

ISBN: 0-595-00388-5

Printed in the United States of America

Contents

Acknowledgments

The author would like to thank Yolanda Henderson, Peter Galbraith, International Public Strategies, Governor Ebrahim Fakhruddin, Mufti Jamiluddin Ahmad, Victoria Schofield, Samiya Waheed, Shahnaz Wazir Ali, Faisal Saleh Hayatt, Mansoor Suhail, Buxial Khan Gudaro, Nancy Powell of the American Embassy, Islamabad; Gillian Peele, Lady Margaret Hall archivist, Oxford University; and Prime Minister Benazir Bhutto for her interview on October 5, 1989. Special thanks to Beth Maynor, Joan F. Smutney, and Betty Barker.

Photos have been provided by Harvard University Archives; Lady Margaret Hall, St. Catherine's College/Oxford University; James Perez/The White House, SIPA Press, and Libby Hughes. Cover photo by Jim Harrison.

Chapter/One

A Child Without Equal

Eight-year-old Benazir Bhutto was trying to sleep in the upstairs bedroom of the Bhutto home at 70 Clifton Road in Karachi, Pakistan. The high, white-washed wall, secured by barbed wire above it, circled the family house and gardens, making the young girl feel safe while her parents were away. A loyal group of servants was there to protect her and her siblings, too, both during the day and at night.

As the final evening chant from the nearby *mosque* (an Islamic place of worship) faded, Benazir reached under her pillow for the money her mother had given her to take care of the house-hold. At bedtime, Benazir had secretly counted the paper *rupees* (Pakistan's currency) and folded her

fingers over them. With her hand beneath the pillow, she clutched the money tightly and drifted off
to sleep.

"Look after the other children. You are the
oldest," had been her mother's parting words to
Benazir as her parents left on another government
trip.

During her parents' absences, Benazir took
charge of her brothers, Mir and Shah, and her sister, Sanam. She was also in charge of the family
home in the busy city of Karachi. This was a serious responsibility. Yet it seemed a natural duty to
Benazir. It would help to shape her future character. At both Harvard University and Oxford University, Benazir took on leadership roles. Perhaps
these early experiences prepared her for an unexpected life in jail. They may also have prepared her
for the responsibilities she assumed in December
1988. At the age of 35, Benazir Bhutto became the
prime minister of Pakistan, and the first woman to
lead a Muslim country.

Pakistan is a small country in Asia. Home to
more than 110 million people today, it is wedged
between Afghanistan and Iran on its western border, and India and China on the east. In the north,
it is capped by the craggy mountains and sparkling
lakes of India's Jammu-Kashmir Province.

Pakistan had been a part of India until August 14, 1947. At that time, India gained its independence from Great Britain. Throughout history, the different religious groups of India—the Hindus and Muslims—had fought bitterly. To try to ease this fighting, East and West Pakistan were created at the same time India became an independent country. The majority of Indian Muslims moved to East and West Pakistan, while almost all Hindus remained in India.

Ali Bhutto, Benazir's father, had been a representative of the young nation of Pakistan since the division. He was often sent out of the country. He served at the United Nations in New York City for seven years. At other times he served Pakistan as its commerce minister, foreign minister, and energy minister. All of these positions required time away from home. Benazir remembers seeing her father more in newspaper photos than in person.

Despite the long absences, Ali Bhutto cared deeply for his children, and he had a great influence on them. The birth of his first child, Mohatarma Benazir, on June 21, 1953, was a very special date in his life. Traditionally, the Muslim world has considered girls less desirable than boys, but not Ali Bhutto. He adored his first-born daughter. He nicknamed her "Pinkie," because, as a baby, her skin was quite rosy and fair. Her given name, though, was to be "Benazir," meaning "without equal" or "without comparison."

Before Benazir's birth, Ali Bhutto had been studying law at Oxford University's Christ Church College in England. His wife, Nusrat, was there with him. Ali Bhutto wanted his child to be born in Pakistan, however, so Nusrat returned to Karachi. He joined her there several months later.

Nusrat Bhutto was Ali Bhutto's second wife. In many Pakistani families, land was kept within the same family for generations by encouraging cousins to wed through an arranged marriage. Ali Bhutto had taken part in this tradition.

At the age of twelve, the young Bhutto was promised a cricket set (a British game similar to baseball) if he would marry a younger cousin. This would keep the Bhutto lands safe within the family. After the ceremonial marriage, Ali did not see his bride again, because he went away to school. Once he had finished high school, his parents sent him to study at the University of California at Berkeley. From there, he continued his studies at Oxford University in England. As an adult, Ali Bhutto saw his first wife only at family gatherings.

A Muslim man is allowed to have four wives,

Benazir Bhutto (third from left) with her family on an official visit with members of the Chinese government in 1963.

as long as he treats and supports all of them fairly. In 1951, Ali Bhutto married Nusrat. This was apparently a happy marriage, as Ali Bhutto never married again. Their marriage was based on equality, and Ali ignored the traditions of eating and sleeping separately from his family.

In many ways, Ali Bhutto was unlike most Muslim men. His early marriage, as well as the time spent studying in the West, made him realize

how unfair many Muslim laws were to women.
This may have been the reason he was attracted to
an untraditional woman such as Nusrat.

Nusrat Bhutto refused to wear the *burqa* when
she appeared in public. A burqa is a large, tent-like
veil which covers a Muslim woman's face and
body. According to Islam, women are expected to
cover themselves whenever they leave their homes,
or when strange men are in the room. Unlike most
Pakistani women at the time, Nusrat Bhutto, who
was born in the neighboring country of Iran, was
college-educated. Before her marriage, she had de-
fied custom by driving her own sports car around
the seaport city of Karachi.

Benazir and her brothers and sisters were born
into this liberated, well-educated family. Ali
Bhutto expected each of his four children to strive
for higher education, too. The education of his
daughters was as important to him as that of his
sons. "I ask only one thing of you, that you do
well in your studies," Bhutto told his children.

Despite Nusrat's own feelings against the veil,
she did not want to impose her feelings on her
daughters. Once, when Benazir was twelve years
old, she and her mother were traveling north by
train from Karachi to Larkana, the site of the family homestead. As they neared the station, Nusrat

unpacked a black burqa and told Benazir she must put it on. "You are no longer a child," she said.

The view of the world from behind the veil was a shock to Benazir. The black veil made all the beautiful colors look gray. The desert heat from behind the curtain was almost unbearable.

"Pinkie wore her burqa for the first time today," Nusrat told Ali later. He was silent for quite a while before he said, "She doesn't need to wear it. The Prophet himself said that the best veil is behind the eyes. Let her be judged by her character and her mind, not by her clothing."

"My father was the dominant role in my life because he was the head of the family," recalls Benazir. "My mother was more like a peer— someone to confide in. We played card games together...I respected her."

Much of Benazir's early life was carefully planned for her by her father. At the age of three, Benazir went to Lady Jennings' nursery school. When she was five years old, she was sent to the Convent of Jesus and Mary, which was down the street from her house in Karachi. Like many upper-class Pakistanis, the Bhuttos felt this private school would offer a better education than a public Muslim school. In the lower grades, Benazir dressed in a simple white dress. In high school, she

Benazir studied in a classroom like this one at the Convent of Jesus and Mary in Karachi.

wore a *shalwar kamiz*, a uniform made up of a white tunic and trousers, draped with a green *dupatta*, or long scarf, from her shoulder across to her waist.

Benazir was given a very good education, and it was in school that she learned much of her English. The languages spoken within the Bhutto home were Sindhi—the language of the province in which they lived; Persian—Nusrat's native language; English; and Urdu—the national language of Pakistan.

Benazir's Urdu teacher at the convent was Humera Naim, who recalled, "Benazir's Urdu was not so good. Her speeches today are well written, and she uses the right words, but she makes some grammatical mistakes in Urdu. I remember when she was fourteen or fifteen that she was very respectful, helpful, polite, and very sweet."

Students at the convent studied between the hours of 7:45 A.M. and 1:15 P.M., with a break for tea or a cold drink and cookies at 10:30. During the break, Benazir might play volleyball outside on the concrete playground. If her father were away, either elsewhere in Pakistan or abroad, he would telephone Benazir to check on her special school reports. In addition to their school-work, Ali Bhutto arranged for tutors to give his children lessons in math and English after school hours.

Despite these full days of serious studying, Benazir always had time to enjoy herself. She liked to play pranks on her teachers, which they recall with much amusement at the convent.

"I remember buying stink bombs in a joke shop in London," Bhutto told the girls at her old school in Karachi in 1987. "The next time we had an exam, I just passed a few of them to my friends. As soon as the exam began, we put them under our chairs and crushed them. There was such a horrible smell that our exams were delayed!"

"I think school has the most dominant influence on a person," Benazir says. "It taught us discipline, perseverance, and how to work under pressure, but there were fun times, too—times of laughter. I remember playing netball and volleyball. I even won a cup for table tennis."

When Ali Bhutto worked for the government, he lived in Rawalpindi in northern Pakistan, near Islamabad, the capital. During this time, Benazir and Sanam were sent to a branch of their Catholic boarding school in nearby Murree. Located in the mountains, Murree had been a British military post at one time, but now belongs to the Pakistan military.

To the two young Bhutto sisters, the cold winds of Murree were very different from the steamy heat of Karachi. Because the school did not have any indoor heating to combat the cold of winter, the school year ran from March through December.

In the Murree school, Benazir slept in a pink dormitory with twenty other girls. Each bed had a doll resting on the pillow. In the morning, Benazir would slip into her white shalwar kamiz with

The dormitory where Bhutto slept while attending school in Murree remains very much the same today.

its red dupatta, brush her bangs and straight hair, and rush down the carpeted metal staircase to breakfast. After eating, she would run down the hillside steps to her classrooms, which overlooked the playing fields for soccer, field hockey, and volleyball.

In 1965, while attending the boarding school, Benazir and Sanam were witness to a war. In 1947, when India was partitioned to form India and

The Convent of Jesus and Mary in the hills of Murree.

Pakistan, the northern area of Jammu-Kashmir was given to India. Since most of the people in the area were Muslims, they felt closer to Pakistan than they did to India. This led to a seventeen-day war between the two countries. The town of Murree, overlooking the valley of Kashmir, was caught in the middle of this conflict. During the many air raids, Benazir and her friends imagined themselves kidnapped and hidden somewhere in the hills.

Benazir's father, then Pakistan's foreign minister, flew to the United Nations to plead for a cease fire. He succeeded. When Pakistan's President Ayub Khan gave Kashmir back to India at a settlement conference, though, Ali Bhutto resigned. He did not think that the president should have agreed with India's plans to keep the province.

In 1967, Ali Bhutto formed his own party, the Pakistan People's Party (PPP). He used his home in Karachi as its headquarters. Angered by this move, Pakistan's president sent Bhutto to jail in the city of Lahore.

Meanwhile, Benazir returned to the Convent of Jesus and Mary in Karachi to finish high school. She remembers herself at the age of fourteen as "very shy—I could hardly lift my eyes off the carpet and say 'hello' to strangers."

Soon, Benazir had to prepare to take her college entrance exams. She wanted to apply to the University of California at Berkeley, where her father had gone as a freshman. Instead, he insisted she go to Radcliffe, a college at Harvard University in Cambridge, Massachusetts.

"The weather in California is too nice," he told her. "The snow and ice in Massachusetts will force you to study."

After applying to Radcliffe, Benazir began to study seriously for her December 1968 exams. She felt lonely in Karachi while her mother and sister were in Lahore visiting her father in jail. But a letter from Ali Bhutto lifted her spirits.

"I am praying for your success in your...examinations," he wrote from prison. "I am really proud to have a daughter who is so bright that she is doing O-levels [entrance exams] at the young age of fifteen, three years before I did them. At this rate, you might become president."

While in solitary confinement in prison, Benazir's father also wrote to tell her she needed to read more. "I know you read a great deal, but you should read a little more of literature and history. Read about Napoleon Bonaparte, the most complete man of modern history. Read about the American Revolution and about Abraham Lincoln ....Read about India from ancient times. And above all, read the history of Islam." She accepted his advice.

After Benazir took her exams that December, she entered the Karachi Grammar School near her home for a term. The time passed slowly as she waited impatiently for the results of her exams to come in the spring.

Chapter/Two

Heading for Harvard

The authorities at Radcliffe College in Cambridge, Massachusetts, were concerned about Benazir Bhutto's age and upbringing. Barely sixteen, she would be coming from the protection of a strict Catholic school. Also, as a member of an upper-class Muslim home, she had been very sheltered. The officials felt that the liberal American society might be too shocking for such a young girl from a Pakistani home. In addition, the country was involved in the Vietnam War at the time. Overall, the college officials did not think it was a good time for Benazir Bhutto to come to America.

Ali Bhutto, however, knew his daughter was level-headed and intelligent. He called upon John Kenneth Galbraith, a one-time ambassador to

India, and an economics professor at Harvard. He asked Galbraith to persuade Radcliffe to allow his daughter into the university.

In the spring of 1969, a letter came from Radcliffe College. Benazir opened it, unsure about the results of her exams, but eager to know the college's decision. Happily, she was accepted.

Leaving her family and friends was hard for Benazir. As she and her mother, who would travel with her, stepped through the carved front door of their home, they uttered a prayer from the *Koran*, the Islamic holy book. The servants crowded around the car, sad to say good-bye to the tall, slim teenager they had protected for sixteen years. When the car left the courtyard and drove past the solid iron gates, Benazir took a final look at her home, trying to memorize its every feature.

As they drove to the airport, Benazir knew she would miss the noisy bustle of Karachi with its 2 million (more than 7 million today) people. Sadly, she realized that she would no longer hear the calls to prayer that echoed through Karachi five times a day. Benazir was frightened because she was leaving the life she knew behind, but excited at the same time.

Mother and daughter arrived at Boston's Logan Airport in the sizzling heat of an August day.

Each day of her life in Pakistan, Benazir heard the calls to prayer from mosques such as this modern one in Karachi.

They were soon crossing the Charles River into Cambridge, to find the Eliot Hall dormitory where Benazir would live.

Nusrat Bhutto spent several weeks helping Benazir settle into her new surroundings. She made sure her daughter had a complete wardrobe, full of Pakistani saris (colorful, loose-fitting dresses) and shalwar kamiz that were tailored in wool for the cold winters.

Before Nusrat left, she and Benazir went to tea at the Galbraith home near the Harvard campus. The Galbraiths would become like second parents to Benazir. She was often invited to their Cambridge home as well as their vacation home in Vermont. Because of his fatherly concern, Professor Galbraith was always available to help and advise Benazir. "John Kenneth Galbraith hovered over Benazir like a father," remembered one of Benazir's friends in later years.

Over tea that day, Benazir met Peter Galbraith, who later became a dear friend. Peter remembers their first meeting. "When she arrived at Harvard, she was a very quiet and shy sixteen-year-old. I had been hitchhiking around South America and proceeded to expound [relate] to them my theories of life at Harvard....After I got through, I expected Mrs. Bhutto would take her daughter back to Pakistan. Of course, I said all this with great authority, but I was barely a freshman and knew absolutely nothing. However, Pinkie did tell me years later that she was shocked at my long, stringy hair."

In fact, coming from a country where the dress code is rather formal, Benazir had a difficult time getting used to the untidy appearance of many young Americans. She found their patched blue jeans, rumpled shirts, and untended beards very strange.

After her mother left, Benazir, using her nickname Pinkie, soon found the college department store, known as the Harvard Coop. There, she bought the "uniform" of the other college students—blue jeans and sweatshirts. Although they were not the traditional clothes of Pakistan, they would let Benazir follow the Muslim custom of completely covering the body. The new outfits also kept her from being too different from her classmates.

Benazir had intended to major in psychology at Radcliffe, but she quickly changed her mind when she found out she would have to perform experiments with animals. This, she could not and would not do. She loved birds and animals, especially her two cats. Therefore, she turned to the president of Radcliffe, Mary Bunting, for some guidance. Benazir decided to major in comparative government—the study of different forms of government. This was good news to her father. He had secretly written to the president, asking her to steer his daughter in the direction of political studies.

Like most teenagers away from home for the first time, Benazir was homesick. Although the autumn leaves of New England were a beautiful sight, she missed the colors of Pakistan, as well

The Charles River flows past Eliot Hall (center), *Bhutto's residence at Radcliffe.*

as her family. Fortunately, the girls near her room befriended her and tried to ease the pain of homesickness.

Anne Fadiman was a friend of Benazir's at Radcliffe. She explained some of the adjustments Benazir had to make in coming from an upper-class Pakistani family. "She had always been chauffeured by a driver; her meals were cooked and served; doing her own laundry was out of the question;

and answering a telephone herself was something new."

Once Benazir learned to do these things and became used to Western ways, she became more outgoing and began to blend into the Harvard University community. Before long, she was elected secretary of Eliot Hall, and was responsible for giving tours to students interested in coming to the university.

Peter Galbraith later recalled, "She was very much a joiner—on the Harvard *Crimson* newspaper. She gave tours. She took part in demonstrations against the Vietnam War. Her first experience with tear gas was not in Pakistan, but on the Boston Common." On the Common with her friends, Benazir stood shouting slogans and holding antiwar signs along with the other protestors.

Not only did Benazir protest against the war, she was attracted to the new women's liberation movement in the United States. At coffee shops and in the dormitory rooms, the Radcliffe girls talked about their new freedom to pursue any career they wanted. If a young woman decided not to marry, this was now considered an acceptable choice. For a Pakistani woman, these views were unusual, as well as brave. Yet, despite Benazir's independence, she would wear traditional Pakistani dress when invited to a function by Pakistani hosts.

With all these exciting outside interests, Benazir never neglected her studies. Keeping her grades high was a part of her promise to her father. She had also been influenced by the hard work required in her Pakistani schools.

"Everything was easy for her. She took care of her academic life without agonizing over it. She was always relaxed and never worried," commented one of Benazir's roommates, Yolanda Henderson.

Meanwhile, in the middle of Benazir's third year at Radcliffe, Pakistan held its first free elections in thirteen years. The voters in West and East Pakistan elected her father and the Pakistan People's Party by a great majority.

In the Pakistani parliamentary system, the prime minister is the head of the government, just as the president is in the United States. The prime minister is the leader of the National Assembly's majority party.

Pakistan also has a president. The president is the head of State and does not have the power of the prime minister. He or she acts more as an adviser. The president can be from either the Senate or the National Assembly. He or she must be elected by the four provincial assemblies, the Senate, and the National Assembly.

When Ali Bhutto became prime minister, Benazir Bhutto became an instant celebrity. When she had first arrived at Radcliffe, no one had known where Pakistan was. A year later, everyone was congratulating her on her father's victory.

Ali Bhutto's success did not last long. Sheik Mujib of East Pakistan demanded independence from West Pakistan. Geographically, the two areas were separated by almost 1,000 miles of India. There was also some disagreement about a new constitution. Sheik Mujib and many of the East Pakistanis felt Pakistani laws were unfair to them. This eventually led to a rebellion.

Benazir's feelings of pride were quickly forgotten when other students began criticizing her country. For almost two years, she defended Pakistan. At the end of 1971, Benazir was shocked when she learned the Indian army had invaded East Pakistan. They had also bombed Karachi and other parts of West Pakistan. The Indian government claimed to be helping East Pakistan gain its independence.

That December, Ali Bhutto flew to the United Nations to challenge India's military attack against Pakistan. He cabled Benazir to ask her to come to New York for sessions with the Security Council. This organization tries to settle disputes be-

Benazir "Pinkie" Bhutto's Radcliffe yearbook photo.

tween nations. Benazir left for New York immediately. Before the Security Council met, Bhutto tested his daughter's thoughts on what the outcome might be.

"All nations will condemn India and make them withdraw their troops from East Pakistan," she said.

With a smile, Ali Bhutto replied, "You may be a good student of international law, Pinkie, but you don't know anything about power politics. One of the fundamental [basic] lessons of diplomacy is to create doubt: Never lay all your cards on the table."

Although the elder Bhutto fought hard in the United Nations Security Council, no decision was made. Losing patience, Ali Bhutto stormed out of the council chamber and returned to Pakistan. Bhutto went back to Harvard. Eventually, East Pakistan became the independent country of Bangladesh.

Because of these events, Benazir Bhutto was gaining much experience. Even her professors noticed a growing maturity and courage. "At eighteen," she remembers, "I was brash and thought I was the cat's whiskers, and I was opinionated."

A senior tutor of Bhutto's, Kevin Starr, witnessed an example of her new boldness. He saw a debate in class between Benazir and a Harvard professor over the rights and wrongs of an independent Bangladesh. Although the students and professor were against her, they admired her courage and the way she stood up for her beliefs. Her reputation soon spread across the campus.

In the beginning of her senior year, Benazir's brother Mir entered Harvard as a freshman. Remembering her own homesickness, Benazir helped Mir meet people and professors. She showed him where everything was at Harvard. When they were together, brother and sister discussed Pakistani politics and read the daily news about their homeland.

During her last year at Harvard, Benazir wrote her senior honors thesis on pink paper, and passed it out to her professors and friends. Although her years in Cambridge had been happy ones, the final days were sad. She had to say good-bye to her friends, some of whom were leaving for graduate school or to start careers.

On graduation day, Benazir's mother and Mir were there to see her graduate *cum laude* (with honors) only days before her twentieth birthday. Although her father could not attend, it was a proud moment for both parents.

Hoping to stay and go to the Fletcher School

of Law and Diplomacy at Tufts University, Benazir pleaded with her father. It was useless. He wanted her to go to Oxford University, where she had already been accepted.

Benazir was happy to be returning to Pakistan for the summer, but sad to be leaving America. She was comforted, though, by the knowledge that Peter Galbraith and his wife would also be attending Oxford University in the fall.

Chapter/Three

On to Oxford

Benazir learned the art of diplomacy—skill in handling disputes peacefully—at her father's side. It was as much a part of her education as her lectures and tests.

One important experience occurred during the summer of her junior year at Harvard. Ali Bhutto invited her to attend a summit. "I want you to witness firsthand a turning point in Pakistan's history," he had told her. This turning point would be a meeting between Prime Minister Indira Gandhi of India and Prime Minister Ali Bhutto. The purpose of the June 1972 meeting was to solve the problems caused by India's military attack of East Pakistan. The two leaders also wanted to end the argument over which country should own Kashmir.

Meeting Prime Minister Gandhi at the parties and receptions was exciting. At dinner, Indira Gandhi stared at Benazir across the table. Perhaps she was remembering the times when she went with her own father, Jawarharlal Nehru, former Indian prime minister, to many different countries.

While Gandhi and Bhutto spent many days negotiating, Benazir wandered around the mountain town of Simla. A group of reporters usually followed her. They commented on the combination of her Pakistani and Harvard wardrobe. It caused quite a stir and was seen as a symbol of the new generation.

Unfortunately, the talks came to a sudden halt. Neither Gandhi nor Bhutto would change their positions. Ali Bhutto told his daughter and advisers to pack and return to Pakistan.

Before leaving, though, Bhutto made one last attempt to make Gandhi change her mind. As a final gesture, the Indian prime minister agreed to give back the territory her nation had taken during the 1971 war, and later the prisoners. In this way, both governments kept their pride.

After the Simla summit, Benazir joined her father on a state visit to the United States in 1973. Ali Bhutto was to be honored at a White House dinner. In the West Room, Bhutto was seated next to Henry Kissinger, secretary of state.

Since Kissinger had been a professor at Harvard before becoming involved in the government, Benazir opened the conversation by talking about some of the problems at the university.

After dinner, Kissinger approached Ali Bhutto and told him, "Mr. Prime Minister, your daughter is even more intimidating [frightening] than you are." Ali Bhutto laughed, proud of his daughter.

This was the kind of training Benazir Bhutto brought with her to Oxford University in the fall of 1973. Ali Bhutto had great respect for Oxford University, and remembered his own years there very well. He wrote this letter to his daughter as she began her university life there. "I felt a strange sensation in imagining you walking on the footprints I left behind at Oxford over twenty-two years ago...Your being at Oxford is a dream come true. We pray and hope that this dream...will grow into a magnificent career in the service of your people."

While Benazir knew her father was happy she was at Oxford, the first months there were hard for her. Her single room at Lady Margaret Hall was small. Unlike her room at Harvard, she had to share a bathroom with the other girls on the floor. Benazir also missed having a private telephone and found the English much more reserved

Lady Margaret Hall, Oxford, where Benazir Bhutto lived from 1973 to 1976.

than the outgoing, friendly Americans. Everyday life, she found out, was harder at Oxford.

However, the pressures of schoolwork kept her busy. She had to write two essays each week for her triple majors of philosophy, politics, and economics. This did not give her time to think about her personal problems. Peter Galbraith and his wife were at Oxford for her first two years, so Benazir was not completely alone.

Benazir's father urged her to join the Oxford Union Debating Society. The debating club is one of the best at the university, dating back to 1823. Benazir was interested in joining the foreign service of Pakistan after graduation, so the debating club seemed a good place to practice her speaking skills. She liked the thrill and challenge of debating. Little did she know, then, that her future life would require all the debating skills she learned at Oxford.

In her formal Pakistani dress, she delivered her first speech at the Oxford Union on the need to impeach, or remove from office, President Richard Nixon. Although Benazir had previously supported President Nixon in his foreign policy, the Watergate investigation changed her attitude. She presented her case so well that the students voted to impeach Nixon 345 to 2. Her debut was a great success.

Benazir's association with the debating club helped her form strong friendships with people such as Victoria Schofield, who would later write a book about Ali Bhutto. With all these interesting activities to keep her busy, Benazir soon became fond of the narrow, winding cobblestone streets of Oxford.

Oxford University was begun in the twelfth

century, when a group of scholars and monks decided to form a college of higher learning. The university is made up of a series of small, self-gov-
erning colleges. The colleges are based on the
tutorial system. Under this system, each student
must write one or two essays a week on each subject, and then discuss them with an individual
tutor. These assignments kept Benazir busy. She
also attended lectures, did research, and was active
in the debating club.

Despite this heavy workload, Benazir did have
some free time. She had a yellow sports car her
father had given her as a graduation present from
Harvard. She could be seen driving the small British MGB convertible around the streets of Oxford.
Often, the windshield was covered with parking
tickets and personal notes from friends. According
to one of her tutors, "That yellow car was her sig-
nature around Oxford. 'There's Benazir Bhutto,'
everyone would say."

On weekends or holidays, she would drive up
to London, only an hour away. Here, she would
treat herself to her favorite peppermint stick ice
cream. At times, she might drive to Stratford-on-
Avon to see a Shakespearean play. Besides these
day trips, there were parties and picnics, boating
on the river, or garden parties at the boathouse.

"She worked hard, played hard, and made lots
of friends," recalls Elizabeth Chilver, principal at
Lady Margaret Hall.

Because of her intelligence and enthusiasm,
Benazir's Oxford tutors thought she might become
an ambassador's assistant at the United Nations.
Yet they did not consider her anything but a nor-
mal student. Her tutor in politics, Gillian Peele, remembers Benazir as "a bubbly sort of character,
charming, and a stylish dresser...She was hardwork-
ing, but it cannot be said she was a perfect...under-
graduate."

Absorbed in the British college life, Benazir
seemed happy. Yet her private thoughts were a little different. "When I became twenty-one," the
prime minister said wistfully, "I was sad to leave
my teenage years in becoming an adult."

As an adult, Benazir found herself having to
deal with adult problems. Before she had left for
America, her father had warned her, "You might
find prejudice in the West." Benazir's first encoun-
ter with racial prejudice came not in America, but
at the London airport.

She had made a quick trip to Pakistan to
attend an Islamic summit planned by her father.
While waiting in line to go through immigration
and customs upon her return to England, the

immigration official made some racial remarks. "How can a Paki have enough money for an Oxford education?" were his parting comments.

Angry and shocked, Benazir refused to reply to his question. She snatched her papers away from him and walked quickly and proudly from the airport. This was her first experience with prejudice, and she began to realize that people saw her country and its residents differently than she did. This attitude both saddened and disappointed her.

Like her time at Harvard, the three years at Oxford passed quickly. This time, though, Benazir was eager to leave school and get started in "real life." But her father insisted she return to Oxford for another year to study international law and diplomacy. Ali Bhutto felt his children must be twice as good as others, because they had had many advantages in life.

Benazir returned to Oxford in 1976. This time, she studied at Saint Catherine's, which had been built in 1962. To Benazir, it did not have the same feeling of history as her old school, Lady Margaret Hall. It did have an interesting mix of foreign students, though. Also, Saint Catherine's offered a degree in international law and diplomacy, which Lady Margaret Hall did not.

Benazir's brother Mir would be a first-year

student at Oxford now, so once again, she had a family member close by. She was also looking forward to her last year at Oxford because she could now campaign for president of the Oxford Union Debating Society. No woman or non-British person had ever been given this honor before.

Changing attitudes toward women had taken a long time to reach the debating society. Ten years before, the ratio of men to women had been seven to one. Despite these odds, Benazir ran for president. She was elected the club's president and began serving the three-month term in January 1977.

After her victory, a cable came from her father. "Overjoyed at your election as president of the Oxford Union," he wrote. "You have done splendidly. Our heartwarming congratulations on your great success."

Before taking on her duties as club president, Benazir and Mir flew home to Pakistan for the winter vacation. The trip began well, with a celebration for Ali Bhutto's birthday at the family home, Al-Murtaza. This one-story house and sprawling gardens were hidden behind high, cream-colored walls and a bright green steel gate near the town of Larkana. In the town, camels and water buffalo lumbered through the winding streets.

At the birthday party, Benazir was introduced

Benazir (front row, center), in formal Pakistani dress, as president of the Oxford Union Debating Society.

At the family home of Al-Murtaza, a picture of Ali Bhutto hangs over the doorway in honor of the former prime minister.

to Zia ul-Haq, who was being considered as her father's chief of staff. After first meeting Zia, Benazir felt uncomfortable. She did not like the way he flattered her. Silently, she wondered why her father had chosen him.

During the party, father and daughter went for a private walk. They strolled under the archways of the sculptured hedges, through the rose gardens, and past the swimming pool and small zoo with its deer and birds. They discussed politics, as they often did. Ali Bhutto told Benazir of his plans to hold elections in March instead of August. He hoped this would help him begin working on the many projects in which he was interested.

One of these projects included equal rights for women in the foreign and civil service. In fact, he had already appointed a few women to important posts. Ali Bhutto also wanted to pass a land reform act, allowing Pakistan's farmers to grow more crops and receive higher pay for them. Overall, he was determined to improve the quality of life for the growing number of poor people in Pakistan. Benazir agreed with her father's plans, and soon flew back to Oxford.

As president of the debating society, Benazir successfully organized and ran four serious debates. When the fifth and final debate arrived, tradition called for it to be light and amusing. A rock and roll musical was the choice. The title was "This House Likes Dominating Women," set to the tune of the song, "Jesus Christ, Superstar," and nicknamed "Bhutto's Bye Bye Song." At the end, Benazir was lifted onto the shoulders of her fellow students and carried out of the hall.

Meanwhile, the political campaign in Pakistan had become violent and emotional. From Oxford, Benazir and Mir listened to radio reports and read the Pakistani newspapers mailed to them. The night

of the March election, they waited for a telephone
call from their father. To their relief, they soon
learned Ali Bhutto had won.

But the post-election riots by the Pakistan
National Alliance (PNA) threatened the country
and Ali Bhutto. Britain's Scotland Yard came to
Oxford at one point and warned Benazir her life
might be in danger, too.

"There was little we could do, in an open site,
to protect her," recalls Principal Chilver. "She was
given her own telephone, so that she could report
anything suspicious, but her best protection was
provided by her fellow students, who kept...watch.
She herself was not alarmed and took the threats
calmly."

Despite these problems, Benazir still felt care-
free enough to celebrate her twenty-fourth birthday by giving a party at Oxford. Ruby red straw-
berries and frothy whipped cream were offered to
her many friends. After this party, Benazir said her
good-byes and returned to Pakistan to join her
family in Rawalpindi. There, she hoped to begin
her diplomatic career by finding a job in one of the
government offices.

Chapter/Four

Caught in a Coup

During the summer of 1977, each of the four Bhutto children returned to Pakistan from various points in the world. They met at their father's official residence, a white mansion set in beautiful grounds in Rawalpindi, near Islamabad.

Islamabad has been the capital of Pakistan since 1959. Once a sleepy mountain village, modern Islamabad has a population of more than 250,000 people. The city has wide boulevards lined with modern office buildings and shops. The four, pencil-thin spires of the Faisal Mosque rise above the skyline. From almost every location in the city, there is a sweeping view of the chalk-white parliamentary buildings. The wood-paneled Senate has a portrait of Mohammed Ali Jinnah—the founder

The parliamentary buildings in Islamabad, capital of Pakistan.

of Pakistan—as its focal point, hung above the speaker of the House. The 80 members of the Senate are elected every six years by the four provinces—each province having an equal number. Its powers are limited. In contrast, the National Assembly, similar to the House of Representatives, has the power to pass laws and approve the budget. There are 237 Assembly members, each of whom serve five-year terms. The number of Assembly members from each province varies according to that province's population.

When Benazir stepped off the airplane in Islamabad and into the arms of her father, he said, "Thank God you've completed your education and are home. Now you can help me." After spending eight years in school, those were the words Benazir wanted to hear. She was now ready to work for her country.

Within a matter of days, Benazir moved into a small office near her father's at the secretariat and began sorting through his files. Considering her education, she was starting in a lowly position. Yet she felt useful and ready to learn as much as she could about the government and her father's political responsibilities.

What seemed like an ideal beginning to her career was about to be destroyed. On the night of July 7, 1977, the Rawalpindi household was suddenly shaken out of a quiet sleep.

"Wake up! Get dressed! Hurry!" Benazir remembers her mother warning. "The army's taken over!"

In a state of fear, Benazir ran to her parents to find out what was happening. Nusrat said that a coup d'etat, or overthrow of the government, by General Zia had taken place.

While Nusrat explained their situation to the rest of the family, Ali Bhutto contacted General Zia. Zia said that he intended to hold another election in ninety days, and that Ali Bhutto was under house arrest. An official car was on its way to the house to take Ali Bhutto to his place of detention.

Shocked by the news, Ali Bhutto thought of his family. He instructed Nusrat and the children to return to the family home in Karachi. Benazir's mother suggested the two boys, Shah and Mir, leave immediately, and perhaps even leave Pakistan. They might be in danger as the sons of the arrested prime minister.

The Bhuttos waited for Zia to come and take the prime minister away. During the long delay, they packed their things. The tense atmosphere was broken by a sharp cry from Nusrat Bhutto. When Benazir and her siblings ran downstairs, they saw Ali Bhutto looking out of the window of a black Mercedes. He was trying to say good-bye. He was soon out of range as the car disappeared through the gates.

The comfortable, safe life of Benazir Bhutto was suddenly in danger. As she stood and watched the car disappear from sight, she recalled the last conversation she had had with her father that evening. He had asked if she believed General Zia would actually hold elections in ninety days as he promised.

"Yes, he will," she had said without hesitation. Her father had called her naive, and explained in harsh words that a government seized by the army did not promise much future for democracy. Zia had ignored the constitution of 1973, and Ali Bhutto thought he would not give up power easily.

General Zia had promised Bhutto he could stay anywhere he desired. This was not the case, however. Bhutto wanted to go to his home in Larkana. Instead, Zia sent him to the colonial rest house in the jagged hills of Murree, where the Bhutto family had spent many vacations. Zia believed that this far-away location would keep Bhutto out of politics. Despite these moves by the new government, both Ali Bhutto and the PPP remained popular.

With General Zia in control of the country, a kind of religious extremism was practiced. During the month of Ramadan, Muslims are not allowed, according to their religion, to eat or drink in public between sunrise and sunset. Normally, if a Muslim breaks this rule, he or she is seen as unfaithful. Zia, though, threatened to arrest and punish anyone who broke their fast.

As expected, the Bhutto family was under a great strain at this time. But for Benazir, at least,

General Zia Ul-Haq.

this experience prepared her for situations she had not encountered before. One lesson she learned was how to deal with journalists. They called the Karachi home constantly for information about her father. Ali Bhutto simply said, "Invite them all to tea."

Following his advice, Benazir asked an eager group of reporters into the crowded dining room, attempting to correct the many rumors that were spreading around Karachi and elsewhere. There was even one rumor that said Ali Bhutto was responsible for the summer rains that were drowning and damaging the farm crops. Another rumor accused Benazir Bhutto of carrying a video camera in her handbag to film illegal political meetings.

During the press conference, Benazir tried to answer as many questions as she could. Later, when talking with her father, she told him of the silly rumors she had heard. He advised her to go immediately to the city of Lahore, where most of the people had suffered ruined crops. This would be a good political move to show that the Bhuttos cared.

Benazir was frightened by his suggestion at first. Yet when she and her brother finally went to Lahore, they were surprised at the overwhelming reception they were given. At one point, Ali Bhutto himself telephoned a public meeting in the city to express his sympathy to all those who had lost crops in the flood.

Because of Ali Bhutto's continued popularity while still in captivity, General Zia decided to release him. The Bhutto family was reunited in Karachi. As happy as Benazir was at their father's freedom, she openly expressed her feelings against Zia. Her father spoke sharply to her about this.

He believed everything they said in their house was being recorded. "You are careless," he told his daughter. "You are not in a democracy of the West now."

The excitement at Bhutto's release was soon overshadowed by Zia's attempts to jail Bhutto again on a false accusation. Benazir was caught in the middle of one of these plots before dawn on a September night in 1977. Five men in white suddenly forced open her bedroom door at the Karachi home and pointed machine guns at her. Not only did they threaten her, but they smashed everything in her room.

Meanwhile, Ali Bhutto was escorted out of the house to military headquarters. Benazir dressed quickly and went with him, despite their attempts to leave her behind. She spoke bravely in her father's defense, but, once again, Ali Bhutto was placed in jail. The judge, however, could not find enough evidence to find him guilty, and Ali Bhutto was set free.

Ali Bhutto was eager to return to campaigning. He warned Benazir again about speaking against Zia when she said, "You're going to win the elections and try General Zia for treason." Since he had told her before about the electronic "bugs," this outburst angered him.

Unfortunately, Ali Bhutto's problems were not over. He was again seized by the army and taken from his house in Larkana. He was put in Sukkur Jail briefly before being moved to Karachi Central Jail, and then to Lahore.

While Ali Bhutto was being moved from jail to jail, Nusrat Bhutto campaigned as a candidate to replace her husband. Such a step is traditional for political families in Asia. Benazir, too, found herself thrust on stage to give speeches. Although frightened by the crowds, she used everything she had learned at Oxford and tried to hide her fear.

Threatened by the popular response to the Bhutto women, Zia placed Benazir under house arrest for fifteen days. Nusrat Bhutto continued to speak out in public, now saying, "My daughter is used to wearing jewelry. Now she will be proud to wear the chains of imprisonment."

During the time she was under house arrest, Benazir burned most of the Bhutto family photos. She did not want the army to find them and use them in any way.

When she was released, Benazir and Nusrat rented a house in Lahore to be near Ali Bhutto during his trial. Benazir became frustrated and angry by the things she heard. The only response

Benazir and Nusrat Bhutto were detained at their home in Karachi for several months at a time.

and comfort were the words from her father. "You can imprison a man, but not an idea."

Further arrests and detentions (being held by the police) awaited Benazir and Nusrat during the trial. At one point, Zia ordered the massacre of any people who supported Bhutto. While facing these hardships, both England and America seemed very far away to young Benazir. All she could do was worry behind the walls of her Karachi home.

At the moment her father was found guilty of murder and sentenced to death, Benazir used her wits to find ways to see him in the Rawalpindi District Jail, and her mother in Lahore. She managed to smuggle messages from Ali Bhutto out of his jail. The messages usually contained advice on how to protest legally against her detention. This advice was rewarded when Benazir was released. Soon after this, though, she had an operation to cure a painful ear infection.

While she was recovering, Benazir's twenty-fifth birthday arrived. To celebrate, she and her mother went to Ali Bhutto's jail. There, Benazir found her father in good spirits, though much thinner than the last time she had seen him. Despite the annoying insects and crawling lizards in the cell, her father teased her and said, "You are twenty-five now and eligible for office." They looked at each other and laughed.

Benazir had decided it was up to her to prepare a legal case to defend her father against the death sentence. To cope with the piles of legal documents, she asked her Oxford friend, Victoria Schofield, to come to Pakistan to help her.

In February 1979, Ali Bhutto delivered a plea in court to remove his death sentence. The plea was denied. Bhutto was sent back to jail despite messages from Great Britain, the United States, and Saudi Arabia on his behalf.

Benazir Bhutto (center) with her Oxford friend Victoria Schofield (left) outside a Pakistani courtroom.

On April 3, 1979, Benazir and her mother were taken to see Ali Bhutto for the last time in the compound of the Rawalpindi Jail. Through the iron bars, the three of them had only thirty minutes to say their good-byes. His last words to Benazir were, "You don't know how much I love you, how much I've always loved you. You are my jewel. You always have been."

The government reported that on April 4, Ali Bhutto was hanged. Benazir, however, believes he may have been killed in some other way because there were no hanging marks on his neck. The real truth may never be known.

As a part of Muslim tradition, Nusrat Bhutto began four months of private mourning. The military would not bother Nusrat, but what of Benazir? She did not know what would happen to her. Whatever it was, she decided she would never give up her father's ideals or his political cause.

Chapter/Five

A Desert Cell

Under heavy guard, Benazir and Nusrat Bhutto were taken to the family burial ground in Larkana to pay their final respects to Ali Bhutto. The grave was only a mound of mud without any identification. Through their tears, the women scattered flower petals over the freshly shoveled mud.

Benazir felt stronger after this emotional event. Everything her father had taught her took on new meaning. "Stand up to the challenge. Fight against overwhelming odds. Overrun the enemy. What you make of your destinies is up to you." These were just a few of his words of advice.

Not long after their visit to the grave and their return to jail, mother and daughter were allowed to go to their home in Karachi. Both women were relieved to be home, where they could once again smell the welcome sea breezes.

With the public mourners for Ali Bhutto crowding into the gardens at 70 Clifton, Benazir began to think about how she could carry out her father's mission. She turned the house into the business headquarters for the PPP. Here, Benazir personally conducted meetings for the party from early in the morning until deep into the night. Party members respected the Bhutto name, so they felt satisfied with Benazir leading the party.

The PPP's efforts to win local elections throughout the country were successful, but the national election against Zia was their main focus. They decided to oppose Zia even without Ali Bhutto. This constant threat of opposition forced Zia to cancel the scheduled elections.

Angry at the continued support for the PPP, Zia moved the Bhutto women to Larkana in 1980 and put them under strict house arrest for six months. This was the seventh time Benazir had been arrested in two years. Although this imprisonment was at Al-Murtaza, they were not allowed to have visitors or to talk on the telephone. Also, any mention of the Bhuttos in newspapers was forbidden by the government. The Bhutto family was still a powerful force in Pakistan. Zia hoped that if their names were not mentioned, people would forget about them.

Within the walls of Al-Murtaza, boredom was Benazir's biggest enemy. Nusrat and Benazir's only contact with the outside world was a shortwave radio that received broadcasts from the British Broadcasting Corporation (BBC). In December 1979, when they heard that Pakistan's neighbor, Afghanistan, had been invaded by the Soviet army, Benazir was stunned. This news deepened her worry about her two brothers. When they had fled Pakistan at the time of the coup, they moved to Afghanistan.

Added to these worries and the increasing boredom, Benazir and Nusrat were facing the first anniversary of Ali Bhutto's death. Their request to visit his grave was denied.

Benazir needed something to keep her busy. She decided to turn all her energies to challenging her six-month detention in court. Her study of law at Oxford, and her father's legal advice in the past, gave her the necessary courage. Benazir and Nusrat were soon free and on their way back to Karachi. Without wasting any time, Benazir became involved in the PPP again. This time, though, Zia's intelligence force followed her and watched her every move.

Benazir continued to have annoying problems

with her ear, which interfered with her political work. She worried about the possibility of deafness. To help Benazir recover, Nusrat suggested her daughter go back to Larkana and take over the running of the family farm. It had been seriously neglected since the coup d'etat almost two years before.

For a woman in Pakistan, this assignment was remarkable. But Benazir had little choice: her father was dead, and her brothers were both hiding in Afghanistan. No Bhutto male could do it. So, Benazir traveled to Larkana and took on a landowner's responsibility. She covered every inch of the flat stretches of land with a jeep and supervised the acres of rice paddies and sugarcane fields.

Benazir's physical and mental problems lessened with these new chores. The people who worked for her had not been managed by a Bhutto family member for two years. Under her direction, the farm prospered.

Pakistani farmland is a rich resource. The 800-mile Indus River nourishes the flat wetlands, where rice and vegetables are grown. On the drier side of the river, cotton and sugar are raised. Benazir was learning firsthand about the problems faced by the farmers.

At the end of a long day in the fields, Benazir

refused to relax. Her evenings were filled with visitors who brought news from the political world, and students who came to speak with her. Many dealt with her as an equal, and she felt she was one of them. Because of her position as a landowner, villagers, too, came to her to settle their personal and marital problems. She disliked making decisions for a married couple, and this was the least favorite part of her job.

Meanwhile, the government was becoming even more strict. Freedom of the press was limited, and political activists were arrested. Nusrat decided the only way to beat Zia in 1980 was for the PPP to unite with a certain section of the opposing party, the PNA. When the two groups came together for discussions, the meeting lasted seven hours. The outcome was called the Movement to Restore Democracy, or the MRD.

Having become very cautious since her father's murder, Benazir distrusted this new organization. But people throughout Pakistan supported the MRD.

The MRD, as well as the continued opposition to his rule, threatened Zia's government. Police broke up a secret meeting of the MRD in the northern part of Punjab Province. There, Nusrat was arrested and sent back to Karachi.

Benazir and her mother had made an agreement

that the two of them would never appear at the same meeting together. After their last detention, Nusrat had said, "There is no use in both of us landing in jail again at the same time, so you keep a low political profile. That way, one of us...can stay on the outside to lead the party."

The military rulers were becoming increasingly frustrated with the MRD and the Bhuttos for encouraging the strikes across the country. On March 7, 1981, police searched for Benazir in Karachi all night and the next day. They even invaded the homes of some of Benazir's closest friends. Some were just questioned, and others were put under house arrest.

On this particular night, Benazir was spending the night at a friend's house while Nusrat held a political meeting at 70 Clifton. In the middle of it, the police forced their way in and arrested Nusrat, demanding to know where Benazir was staying. She would not tell them.

As they searched throughout Karachi, the police located Benazir the next day at the home of Nusrat Bhutto's doctor. Benazir was later to learn that Zia had not only arrested her, but six thousand MRD supporters as well.

Not knowing what would happen to her, Benazir was sent to Karachi Central Jail. Five hours

The Karachi Central Jail, one of several prisons in which Bhutto was held during Zia's reign.

later, she learned that her own mother had been placed in a cell without any running water or bedding.

Benazir was kept five days in this jail. On March 13, 1981, in an attempt to frighten her, the police drove her through Karachi to the airport with the sounds of screaming sirens. She was put on an airplane without any explanation as to why and where she was going. On board, she was given a newspaper to read. One of the articles reported that a Pakistani airplane had been hijacked in Afghanistan, and the hijackers were demanding the release of fifty-five Pakistani politial prisoners. One military man and one passenger were shot before the plane was forced to fly to Syria. The article suggested her brother Mir had planned the hijacking. Terrified, Benazir finally understood why she and her mother were being treated as they were. General Zia and the military thought the Bhutto women were involved in planning the hijacking.

Benazir was flown out of Karachi to Sukkur Jail, far away in the Thar Desert. Here, her cell seemed more like a cage, with barred doors on two sides and barred windows on four sides. At night, there was no electricity, and she shivered as the cold winds swept across the desert and whipped through the open bars of her cell. Without blankets or warm clothing, the cold bothered her, making it hard to sleep on the rope cot.

Being separated from people and other prisoners made her feel ill and depressed. She decided she must find things to do to keep herself occupied. Everything Benazir did, from brushing her hair to brushing her teeth, had a set routine. This way, each moment of the day had a purpose.

Benazir did not like the prison food. She was

given watery soup and tea with some bread. Sometimes, the guards offered her pumpkin or fish. Finally, unable even to try to eat the food, she stopped eating altogether.

To avoid the long hours with nothing to do, Benazir began keeping a daily diary in a small notebook. It had been secretly given to her by a sympathetic jailkeeper. Carefully, she recorded events inside and outside the prison. Fortunately, some of her jailers could be trusted. They took the notes away every day and hid them safely. Benazir was also allowed to read one newspaper every day, which she read over and over again.

Each day, her captors warned her of a possible trial and death sentence. During the five months she spent in Sukkur Jail, Benazir continued to grow thinner. Worried that she might die in jail, the police shifted her back to the Karachi Central Jail, where she hoped to see her mother. Instead, she was pushed into a dark, dirty cell. To her surprise, she was taken to a hospital the next day. The guards said she had uterine cancer. She had known nothing about this, and had not given her consent for an operation.

At the hospital, Sanam was permitted to visit her for thirty minutes. She found Benazir drugged, screaming about her father's death, and fears of her own death.

Bhutto's cell in Sukkur Jail.

Two days after her operation, Benazir was flown back to Sukkur Jail. Years later, Benazir heard that a former Pakistani minister in the PPP received a telephone call in London about the government's attempt to kill Benazir Bhutto on the operating table. The minister immediately gave a press conference and reported this information to the London newspapers. Benazir does not know for certain if her death was Zia's intent, but she feels sure the public attention helped to save her life.

Meanwhile, the Pakistani newspapers were making terrible accusations against Mir and Shah for heading a secret organization called Al-Zulkifar from Afghanistan. The articles also claimed that Nusrat and Benazir knew about this. Benazir was angered, especially when she heard that Zia was arresting and torturing those who had any connection to the name of Bhutto.

Within her jail cell, Benazir was suffering from a different kind of torture. The daytime heat in May soared to 120°F (48°C). The hot desert dust swirled into her cell, crusting her face. Her skin cracked and peeled, and unsightly blisters appeared on her face. Without the proper diet, her hair began to fall out in clumps, too.

At this point, Benazir says her jail officials began suggesting suicide as a way to end her physical suffering. They told her that her party leaders and followers were deserting her. "I prayed to God to give me strength," she said later. To her jailers, she said, "If I am the only person left resisting the tyranny of the regime, then so be it. I don't believe your lies."

In this weakened condition, Benazir celebrated her twenty-eighth birthday. Her sister Sanam was the only visitor. Sanam brought some happy news at last—she planned to marry Nasser Hussein, a longtime friend of their brothers. Benazir could not have been happier for her sister, feeling that this step would help protect her. Nasser had a successful telecommunications business, and Benazir thought he was a good person.

After Sanam had left, Benazir turned to prayer. Each day she hoped for a miracle. Then one day, the matron of the jail opened the gate to her cell and told Benazir she was leaving.

For a moment, Benazir was hopeful. Perhaps she would at last be allowed to return to her home in Karachi. There, she would see her mother, who had been sent home recently after having been found coughing up blood in her Karachi cell.

The police vehicles screeched out of Sukkur Jail, sped over the canal locks, and raced along the crumbling tarmac to Sukkur airport, where Benazir was placed on a plane to Karachi. There, she was met by army vehicles that passed the turn-off to her home, dashing her hopes for a family reunion.

Chapter/Six

Jailed and Alone

The army convoy switched on their sirens to force their way through the traffic of Karachi until they drove into the familiar compound of dried, baked earth. Ahead was the Central Jail, a sturdy looking fortress trimmed in blue. There, Benazir entered the first iron gate and climbed through a hole in the red and blue steel door into a dark hall. This led to the superintendent's office. From there, she squeezed through another hole into an open-walled compound. She was pushed through the final gate into a cell that had once held her own mother. The feeling of depression on that August day in 1981 was almost more than she could bear.

Benazir's cell was inside a locked courtyard. All the prisoners had been moved out of the adjoining cells, leaving her alone except for a jail matron. The cell was smaller than the one at Sukkur Jail. The walls were peeling, and the ceiling fan didn't work. Only the barred windows gave off limited light and air. Benazir could hardly breathe from the wet heat of the Karachi summer.

"Sometimes in jail," she recalls, "I would indulge in self-pity and say to myself, 'Why do I have to suffer so much?' Then, I would feel guilty and focus on God and be grateful. I used to cry in my pillow at night."

The dead silence at night was even more frightening than being locked in jail. After sunset, she thought she heard noises and voices, but her guards told her she was imagining the sounds. These words reminded her of her father's jail terms. People had walked on the roof of his cell, attempting to break his calm and make him think he was going mad. Once Benazir realized this, she began praying regularly, trying to ignore all of the sounds. They eventually stopped.

Longing to see her mother, Benazir was finally allowed a short visit from her. She was shocked at Nusrat Bhutto's appearance. Benazir had remembered her mother as elegant and beautiful, not as this thin, old woman with gray hair. Because of the listening guards, the two women talked mostly about Nusrat's health. According to the doctors, she was suffering from either tuberculosis—a lung disease—or lung cancer.

After Nusrat left, Benazir felt even more lonely than she had before. She began to think about her family's misfortunes: she was in solitary confinement, her father was dead, her mother was ill, and her two brothers were somewhere in a distant land.

The only way to dismiss these thoughts of self-pity was to focus on events outside her world. She did this by reading newspapers. From them, she learned that the United States was now taking notice of Pakistan because of the Soviet invasion into Afghanistan. Before this, the U.S. government had withdrawn aid from Pakistan for fear it was developing its own nuclear bomb.

When Ronald Reagan defeated Jimmy Carter in the 1980 presidential elections, the U.S. government began providing money to Pakistan again. In order to prevent the Soviet forces from pushing over the borders into Pakistan, the United States supplied General Zia with millions of dollars and supplies. Reportedly, Zia kept large amounts of this aid for himself. He told the world that Pakistan was fighting communism. A spokesperson for the American State Department called him a "world

When Benazir was held in this cell in 1980, it contained nothing but a bare cot.

statesman" and a "benevolent [kindly] dictator." Further aid came from international food organizations to help support the Afghan refugees entering Pakistan.

As Benazir sat in her cell and read about Zia becoming a hero in the eyes of the Western world, she was torn between discouragement and anger. Unable to think about the political situation in Pakistan without becoming enraged, Benazir tried to concentrate on her sister's wedding. It would be held in Karachi on September 8, 1981. The jail

superintendent offered to free her for the wedding
if she would give up politics completely. Benazir
refused.

On the evening of the wedding, the prison matron came to Benazir suddenly and told her she
had permission to go to Sanam's wedding. In a
daze, Benazir was taken in a train of police cars to
70 Clifton. As she stepped into the courtyard at
the front entrance, she was greeted with the scent
of jasmine and roses, and the sounds of festive
music. Her relatives, who had come from as far as
California, England, France, and all parts of Pakistan, rushed to embrace her.

Benazir's first step was to take a hot bath. As
she tried to wash away the grime from weeks in
her unsanitary cell, she began to put aside the
hardships of jail. Sipping the pure, cold water was
another luxury she had missed.

Benazir spent the next two days reading international and national publications, and talking with
her mother and sister. Benazir was happy that
Sanam's was not an arranged marriage, as was typical in Pakistan. Nasser Hussein had risked the dis-
pleasure of his family in marrying Sanam. They
considered the Bhutto name a dangerous one.
Nasser and Sanam had stood up for themselves,
though, and Benazir was very glad for them.

As part of the traditional wedding ceremony, the reddish brown henna dye, called *mehndi*, was used to paint beautiful scrolls and pictures on the hands and feet of the ladies. Under a canopy, the wedding couple sat on cushions inlaid with tiny sparkling mirrors. The guests chanted songs about the conditions of the marriage, and what each partner would do for the other.

The police interrupted the ceremonies several times, serving notices to Nusrat and, in general, trying to upset the Bhutto family. Benazir had become so used to their methods and to her life in prison that she caught herself referring to the jail as her home.

Ignoring the police disturbances, the wedding continued. The bride and groom were each asked three times if they agreed to the marriage. At the end of the marriage vows, the couple looked into a mirror placed between them to recognize their new married state. Watching them, Benazir felt her eyes fill with tears.

When the ceremony was over, Benazir hastily wrote a letter to Peter Galbraith, her friend from Harvard and Oxford. She had learned during the wedding that he had come to Pakistan, demanding to see her in jail. He had carried with him a letter from the Senate Foreign Relations Committee which also asked that he be allowed to see her. He was turned down, but had returned to the United States determined to help the Bhutto women.

Benazir's letter to Peter Galbraith said, among other things, "Did they teach us that life could be full of such terrible dangers and tragedies....Freedom and liberty, the essays we wrote on them, papers for our tutors, for grades, but did we know the value of those words which we bandied about, or how precious they are, as precious as the air we breathe, the water we drink."

Finally, the wedding celebration was over, and Benazir was taken back to jail. This time, she was taken to a smaller, darker cell. There, she would read, write, and think about her country and its future.

On December 11, 1981, the deputy superintendent came to Benazir's cell and told her to pack her belongings. She would be taken to Larkana the next morning under police escort. Strangely enough, Benazir was sad to leave the Karachi Central Jail. At least she knew what to expect there.

The next day she was driven to her family home, Al-Murtaza. She was told she would be free to use the telephone and have visitors. Her happiness at this news did not last long. The only visitors she could have were a few relatives. She was allowed no telephone calls, except to and from relatives. She tried to learn how to cook to make the long, dull days pass quickly.

Along with these difficulties came news that Nusrat Bhutto's health was not good. In fact, news that she had cancer had been leaked to reporters in London and other cities. This resulted in another campaign to "save the Bhutto ladies." Zia, however, did not want Nusrat to leave Pakistan. He directed her doctor to sign a report claiming that further medical treatment was not necessary. Risking his personal safety, Nusrat's physician refused to follow Zia's orders, as did all the doctors on the medical board.

On November 20, 1982, Nusrat was allowed to travel to West Germany and Switzerland for medical treatment. To say farewell to her mother, Benazir was driven under heavy military guard to the airport, and flown to Karachi after eleven months in Larkana.

Feeling lonely, Benazir parted from her mother at 70 Clifton. Instead of returning to Larkana, Benazir was placed under house arrest in Karachi for another fourteen months.

In December 1982, General Zia made an official visit to the United States to meet with President Ronald Reagan. There, the Senate Foreign Relations

Committee challenged him with the reported abuse
of political prisoners in Pakistan. When they demanded to know the location of Benazir Bhutto,
he lost his temper and said, "I can tell you she
lives in a better house than any senator and is allowed visitors and can use the telephone."

To challenge that statement, Peter Galbraith
telephoned the Bhutto residence in Karachi and
asked to speak to Benazir. "You cannot speak to
her. It is forbidden," was the answer. Even after
identifying himself and saying he had President
Zia's permission, the guards refused to let him
speak to her.

Unaware of these efforts, Benazir began 1983
ill and tense. She began grinding her teeth at night,
and woke to find her knuckles swollen. The problems with her ear returned, too, and would not go
away. To try to ease the pain and isolation, she
prayed daily to God.

Meanwhile, the Senate Foreign Relations Committee, under the constant pressure of Peter Galbraith, kept asking Pakistan about Benazir Bhutto's
confinement. The committee personally asked Pakistan's foreign minister on his Washington visit
about Bhutto's treatment. He was shocked by the
facts they presented to him, and promised to in-
vestigate immediately.

Despite her physical problems, Benazir was encouraged by news that the Movement to Restore Democracy (MRD) was still resisting the military. Taking heart from this news, Benazir wrote encouraging letters to the group with her mother's name on them. She did not want to use her own name for fear she would be punished for taking part in illegal activities. She thought that her mother, now living in Europe, would be safe from any punishment.

By June 1983, the infection in Benazir's ear was constant. Her doctor told the authorities that Benazir needed special treatment in Europe. In December, the government granted her permission to go to Switzerland for surgery. When they gave her the news, Benazir could hardly believe it. She was afraid to show any emotion or excitement. Her feelings, after seven years, had become numb.

Chapter/Seven

Politics in Exile

In January 1984, Benazir Bhutto stepped from the airplane onto the runway in Geneva, Switzerland. Her eyes, used to darkness from her years in prison, squinted in the blinding sunlight. Her mother was there to greet her and Sanam. "Yesterday, I was a prisoner. Today, I am free with my mother and sister. We are together. We are all alive," Benazir said gratefully.

The reunion was a very happy one, interrupted by telephone calls from relatives and well-wishers. Benazir's brother Mir, who was living in Switzerland, came to see her with his little daughter, eighteen-month-old Fathi. Mir, now twenty-nine, was handsome and gentle. Her other brother, Shah, could not come from the south of France to meet her. The last time she had seen him, he had been eighteen years old. He was now twenty-five.

As much as Benazir wanted to stay close to her reunited family, she needed to go to London for medical treatment. She also wanted to continue her political opposition to Zia. This she could do in England. At that time, there were already 378,000 Pakistanis living in the country.

Sanam, who now lived in London with her husband, traveled with Benazir to London's Heathrow Airport. Word had spread among the Pakistani community of her arrival, and a large crowd awaited her. Strangers thought Benazir was a movie star. When they learned she was a political leader, they asked if she was going into exile.

"I was born in Pakistan and I'm going to die in Pakistan," she replied. To her fellow Pakistanis, she said, "I am not giving up on you. I will stay by your side until my last breath. The Bhuttos keep their promises."

For a short while, Benazir was a guest at her Aunt Behjat's apartment in London's Knightsbridge section. The telephone never stopped ringing, and visitors streamed through the apartment at all hours. But when a car, filled with Pakistani men, began following Benazir wherever she went, she

After her release from prison, Benazir was able to see her brother Mir for the first time in seven years.

became suspicious. Her aunt called Scotland Yard, the detective department of the London police. The car soon vanished from in front of the apartment building.

Benazir had difficulties adjusting to her freedom. A fear of crowds, and of being followed, bothered her. Even the closed-in feeling of the underground subway kept her above ground, using taxis for all her travel. Not wanting to disappoint the Pakistanis who looked to her as a strong figure, she kept these fears to herself.

Shortly after her arrival in London, Peter Galbraith arrived and met with Benazir. He had flown to Pakistan to try to see her, but found out she had already been released. He had not seen her since 1977, and noticed that she had a new self-confidence. They discussed the personal changes in their lives and those of their friends.

Peter tried to persuade Benazir to go to America and apply for a fellowship at Harvard. "My first obligation is to the party. In political terms, it makes more sense for me to be here, where the Pakistani community is larger," she replied.

Finally, in late January, Benazir underwent surgery on her ear. The doctors told her it would take nine months for her to recover. Nusrat Bhutto's health had greatly improved since she left Pakistan. She now came from Switzerland and rented an apartment in the London suburbs where she could help restore her daughter's health.

During these long months, Benazir developed a plan to wage a publicity campaign in the international press. She wanted to expose the cruel treatment of 40,000 political prisoners held in Pakistan. She began by providing specific information to Amnesty International, a worldwide organization that seeks to have political prisoners freed.

As a result of these efforts, the Carnegie Endowment for International Peace in Washington, D.C., invited Bhutto to speak in March 1984. With her girlhood friend Yasmin Niazi, she flew to the United States to speak for the Carnegie Endowment. She also visited senators and State Department officials. She asked for their public support in demanding the release of political prisoners in Pakistan.

In the Senate Foreign Relations Committee, they asked her if aid to Pakistan should be stopped. As much as Bhutto was opposed to Zia's policies, she answered by saying, "Cutting off aid will only create misunderstandings between our two countries. Both our countries would be better served if aid were linked to the restoration of human rights and democracy to Pakistan." The committee decided to continue aid to Pakistan.

Upon returning to England, Bhutto found an apartment to rent near Saint Paul's Cathedral. It had security guards, which reduced her fear of unwanted visitors, and let her check the people coming and going. The small apartment became the headquarters for the Pakistan People's Party (PPP) abroad.

Once again, Bhutto increased her efforts to save her country's political prisoners. Her first effort was to produce a news magazine in both Urdu and English. Benazir also traveled all over England and other parts of Europe, speaking to Pakistani groups. She slowly established a small, but growing, opposition to Zia.

Faced with this threat, Zia sentenced many prisoners to death. Benazir protested these executions by appealing to Elliot Abrams, the assistant secretary of state for human rights. She also spoke to members of Parliament.

United States government leaders, too, began to put pressure on Zia. They insisted he hold general elections in Pakistan, which he agreed to schedule for March 1985. But first, he announced a referendum for December 20, 1984. This would give the people of Pakistan an opportunity to say whether or not they wanted elections to be held. Zia told the Pakistanis that a vote for general elections would be a vote against Islam.

Through their news magazine and a secret organization in Pakistan and abroad, Benazir Bhutto and the PPP attempted to inform voters about the referendum. They urged people to boycott the vote. The Manchester *Guardian*, a London newspaper, later reported that only 10 percent of

Pakistanis had voted. The government, however, claimed 64 percent had voted.

After the referendum, general elections were scheduled for March. PPP leaders suggested that Benazir Bhutto return to Pakistan to challenge Zia. The suggestion was soon dismissed when Benazir learned that her Karachi home was surrounded by the army. A warrant for the arrest of Nusrat and Benazir had been issued.

The March election was held, and Zia won—although the turnout was again very low. Zia then announced that he would change his government from a military to a civilian government.

Sadly, the execution of political prisoners continued. Frustrated, Benazir Bhutto spoke out publicly. She spoke at Harvard in 1985, addressing the Council on Foreign Relations. She also delivered a speech to the members of the European Parliament in Strasbourg.

At Strasbourg, she said, "When the conscience of the world is justly aroused against apartheid and against human rights violations...then that conscience ought not to close its eyes to the murder by military courts which takes place in a country which receives...aid from the West itself." Following this speech, more than 54 prisoners in Lahore were sentenced to death.

After her exile to England, Bhutto spoke before the Council on Foreign Relations about the troubles in Pakistan.

In mid-1985, Benazir felt she needed a break from the constant pressures of politics. She arranged a vacation with members of her family in the south of France.

After her plane landed in Cannes, Benazir looked around for someone to meet her. There was no one. Suddenly, her brother Shah jumped out from behind a pillar to surprise her. The other family members came out from their hiding places, too. Benazir was very happy to see her youngest brother.

Shah had always had a special fondness for Benazir. He had written to her frequently when she had first left home to go to Harvard. Later, Ali Bhutto had sent Shah away to military school. He thought his mischievous young son needed to learn some discipline. For Shah, it was a very unhappy experience. He had pleaded with his mother to let him return to Islamabad and attend the International School there. She had finally agreed. Not only did Shah like to play pranks, he was very generous. If someone asked him for his coat, he would give it away to them.

After Mir and Shah had escaped to Afghanistan at the time of the coup, they met and married sisters. Mir and Fauzia had eventually moved to Switzerland. Shah and his wife, Rehana, had a daughter named Sassi and were now living in

Cannes. Unfortunately, Shah's marriage was not a happy one, and the couple only stayed together for the sake of their daughter.

Knowing this, Benazir was not surprised when Shah told her he intended to divorce his wife. Nevertheless, Benazir pleaded with him to make every effort to remain together. She also tried to befriend Rehana during her month-long stay in Cannes, but found the other woman to be somewhat unfriendly.

On the morning Shah had planned to take Benazir to Nice, in southern France, the two Bhutto women received a disturbing phone call from Rehana. Something was wrong with Shah, she told them. He had taken poison.

What followed seemed a nightmare to Benazir. When she and Nusrat arrived at Shah's apartment, they found him dead on the living room floor. Although the official explanation was suicide, many people suspected a political murder.

Against the advice of friends and relatives, Benazir decided in August 1985 to take the body of her brother back to the family grave in Larkana, Pakistan. The Pakistani military leaders were not pleased with this decision, yet they could not stop the burial. Worldwide publicity and pressure would be bad for the current government.

Bhutto returned to Pakistan briefly in 1985 to bury Shah. Mourners filled the streets, causing traffic jams.

The mourners crowded into Larkana and Karachi. Once again, the government detained Benazir. But this time, the U.S. State Department protested. In an official statement, a spokesperson said, "Pakistan has taken encouraging steps toward... constitutional government....Putting Ms. Bhutto under house arrest would appear...inconsistent with this process."

Meanwhile, Rehana had been arrested in connection with Shah's death, and Benazir had been asked to appear in court. In November, she was allowed to leave Pakistan to testify in Nice, France. Due to the suspicions against Rehana, Mir and Fauzia had separated.

Eventually, Sassi, Shah's daughter, was sent to live with grandparents in the United States. To this day, the Bhuttos do not know where she is. They refuse to give up hope, though, because Sassi's name means, "one who crosses the deserts and mountains to find the family who loves her."

"Difficulty is a part of everyday life," says Benazir Bhutto when remembering this period of her life. "I took my father for granted and lost him. My brother was so young when he died—and in a safe place like France. Suddenly, when those who are closest to you are gone, you think of all those unspoken words. We don't appreciate our mothers and fathers, and the gift they are to you."

Chapter/Eight

A Heroine Returns

Toward the end of 1985, Bhutto traveled throughout Europe to speak to groups of Pakistanis. She inspired them with the promise of restoring democracy in Pakistan. During one of these rallies, she heard that martial law had been lifted.

Bhutto was immediately suspicious. Her past experience with General Zia made her doubt his promises. She learned that before the civilian government took office, many organizers in the opposition party were arrested and sentenced to long jail terms. In this way, Zia removed the "troublemakers."

Despite Zia's step to move away from military rule, Benazir reminded everyone that democracy had all but disappeared since Ali Bhutto's death.

Crime and corruption (dishonesty), especially in the cities, had risen. Since 1979, when the Soviet Union had invaded Afghanistan, refugees from that country had been fleeing to Pakistan. Money and weapons, coming from the United States to help the Afghan fighters and refugees, found their way into the Pakistani black market. This meant those guns and rifles were for sale in the public bazaars, or marketplaces, of Pakistan. The drug problem, too, was beyond control. Farmers used their fields to grow poppies (used in making heroin) instead of food crops.

Also during his rule, Zia had used some of the more extreme ideas of the Islamic religion to support his political policies. One of these was to limit the freedom of women. *Mullahs*, Muslim religious leaders, insisted that all women in Pakistan wear the traditional Pakistani dress in public at all times. Also, if a woman were even suspected of being unfaithful to her husband, she could be jailed and stoned to death. By 1989, most of the prisoners in the Karachi Central Jail were women.

Zia, though, did not expect the behavior that resulted from these harsh religious laws. Violence increased throughout the country, not only men against women, but province against province, and man against man. No one liked the religious tax placed on personal income, either.

Because of the violent conditions growing within Pakistan, Benazir Bhutto met with fellow party leaders in her London apartment. They discussed her future, as well as Pakistan's future.

In January 1986, Benazir made an announcement. "I'm going home," she told members of the PPP. Instead of rejecting this decision, they agreed with her. Most felt it was time she went back. Although her personal safety would be at risk, events around the world pointed toward a spread of democracy. Dictators had been overthrown in Haiti and the Philippines, and many felt it was Pakistan's turn.

In London, the PPP leaders carefully planned Bhutto's trip. As they decided upon their strategy, rumors spread about her possible return. The Bhuttos received messages telling her not to return, that she would be killed. People telephoned in the middle of the night, threatening to stop her.

Bhutto refused to be frightened by these threats. She flew to the United States for discussions with American senators and representatives of the Democratic party in Congress. She believed that their public support would insure her safety and protection.

Yet her greatest security would be the international media. They were attracted to the story of a beautiful young woman leading her followers to freedom. Reporters and television cameras covered and publicized her every move, from Washington, to London, to Mecca, where Muslims make a spiritual pilgrimage. At Mecca, Bhutto's prayers prepared her for the challenge ahead.

Finally, a date was chosen for her arrival in Lahore. Although confident about her decision, Benazir was worried. Would her people welcome her, or would they be afraid of the police? She feared that they might be angry with her, or would not care about her return.

As the airplane circled for its landing at dawn, Benazir and her colleagues stared out the windows in surprise. The runway and surrounding areas of the airport were thick with the bobbing heads of people. Over the loudspeaker, the pilot said, "We welcome Miss Benazir Bhutto back to Pakistan." From the air controllers, the pilot received word that a million people were on the ground to greet Benazir Bhutto.

Benazir was shocked at the huge crowd awaiting her. When her feet finally touched the land of her birth, she knew she was where she belonged. The sweet smell of jasmine in the air brought back

Bhutto spoke before hundreds of thousands of supporters in Lahore.

familiar memories. For a brief moment, she felt a
touch of sadness for her father. These memories
were soon set aside, however, in the crush of the
crowd. The people greeted her with chants of
"Live, live, Bhutto live!" and "Benazir has come,
revolution has come!"

Benazir was quickly pushed onto the deck of a
truck. She stood on a platform, waving to the
masses of people. From there, they would be able

to see her on the way to the Minar-i-Pakistan
monument. This monument had special meaning
for Benazir. Her father had authorized it to be built
as a symbol of Pakistan's birth. Although only
minutes away from the airport normally, it took
ten hours to reach because the crowd swelled to 3
million.

Showers of rose petals and balloons filled the
air, adding to the festive and noisy atmosphere. By
the time the truck reached the monument, it was
dusk. Benazir stepped onto the specially erected
stage to the sound of cheers.

The crowd quieted as she began to speak.
"Here and now," she told the waiting Pakistanis, "I
vow I will make every sacrifice to secure people's
rights. Do you want freedom? Do you want democracy? Do you want a revolution?" Each time, the
people responded with a loud "yes."

"I put an end to revenge. I don't have any
such feelings in my heart. I want to build Pakistan," she continued. The crowd responded by saying, "Zia must go."

There were threatening incidents during her
stay in Lahore. Everywhere Bhutto went, she spoke
of her democratic dream for Pakistan. "People
think I am weak because I am a woman. Do they
know I am a Muslim woman, and that the Muslim

A political poster showing Benazir and her father, Ali Bhutto, reminds voters of the Bhuttos' promise of democracy.

women have a heritage to be proud of?" she asked.

Bhutto left her mark throughout Pakistan. In the northern Punjab province, the police presented her with a restraining order. Thinking she would ignore it, they were ready to arrest her. Instead, she returned to Karachi, and her home at 70 Clifton.

There, she prepared to celebrate Pakistan's Independence Day on August 14, 1986, with the MRD and PPP. The foreign press arrived, including her Harvard classmate, Anne Fadiman.

On Independence day, Fadiman recorded the events of Bhutto's day. She desecribed Bhutto's morning prayer within the doors of her home, and the dusty sport stadium in Lyari, where 10,000 people waited for Bhutto's arrival.

Inside the stadium, the people chanted, "We'll beat them; we'll die; but we'll bring Benazir," over and over again. Before Bhutto could reach the place from where she would speak, though, the police sprayed the air with tear gas. As they followed her van and came closer, she escaped to a cab. It took her home while the police were led on a false trail by a friend wearing her dupatta.

Not long after this, the police arrested Bhutto and placed her in solitary confinement in Landhi Borstal Jail on the outskirts of Karachi; the Central Jail was full of political prisoners. There she stayed until she was freed in September. Although free, there were now assassination attempts on Bhutto's life. To be safe, she often made three different plans for every trip to keep her enemies guessing. To Benazir, it seemed as if the struggle had just begun.

Chapter/Nine

Serving the Nation

In the summer of 1987, Benazir Bhutto made an announcement that pleased Zia's government, and worried some of her supporters. She planned to marry. Because of this, Zia decided to hold elections one year earlier than scheduled. He hoped the people would think her marriage would force her out of politics.

Although Bhutto was not a traditional Pakistani woman, she had agreed to an arranged marriage. This was due partly to the unusual set of circumstances in her public life. She explained to her Radcliffe classmate, Anne Fadiman. "For me, the choice was not between a love marriage and an arranged marriage, but between an arranged marriage and no marriage. It simply would not be possible for me to have a date or get to know a man the way you could. Even the hint of a relationship would have been used by my opponents to destroy me politically."

Nusrat Bhutto had been trying to arrange a marriage for her daughter since Benazir's graduation from Radcliffe. Again and again, Benazir resisted the idea. After her father's death, marriage was definitely set aside. When she was imprisoned, detained, and exiled to England, marriage could not even be considered. Also, Benazir wondered if a man could live her kind of life—the constant travel and political meetings. The Pakistani people would have to come first, not a husband.

In addition, her time in prison had made her frightened of sudden noises, and very nervous around people—even her family. When her mother had pressed her on the subject of an arranged marriage, Bhutto had said, "I have to find myself before I am ready to marry. I have to find a relative calm. I need time to recover."

Despite all these protests, a single woman in a Muslim country could have a very difficult time. Realizing this, Nusrat Bhutto, an untraditional Muslim woman herself, had begun searching for a suitable husband for Benazir in 1985. With the help of Benazir's aunts, they chose a young man of Benazir's age. He came from the Sindh Province, too, and was from a wealthy, landowning family. Asif Ali Zardari had studied at the London Centre of Economic and Political Studies and was very athletic, especially as a polo player. Asif had been brought to Benazir's aunt's house for inspection. Nusrat approved. But before she could tell Benazir, Shah had died. With this tragic news, marriage was once again out of the question.

In February 1987, Bhutto flew to England to appear on a television panel discussion about Afghanistan. Once there, the subject of marriage came up again. Bhutto's aunt and mother continued to press her about meeting Asif. His stepmother had even come to London to speak to the Bhutto women about him.

Still afraid of taking this step, Bhutto pleaded with her mother, asking to wait until June to make a decision. But back in Karachi, Asif's stepmother approached Benazir directly at a meeting at the 70 Clifton home.

"My politics are a commitment to freedom and the meaning of life," Benazir told the woman. "How would a man feel, knowing that his wife's life does not revolve around him?"

"My dear," the stepmother replied, "Asif is a

very confident young man. He knows what he is in for."

In July 1987, Bhutto returned to London. At a brief social meeting in the living room of her aunt's apartment, surrounded by relatives, she met Asif Zardari. Although they did not speak directly to each other, the next day Asif sent Benazir roses. Mangoes and candy arrived the following day.

Yet Benazir was still unsure, and would not give her mother an answer. She made her decision a few days later. At a social gathering, Benazir was stung by a bee. Asif insisted he drive her to the hospital. She was impressed with his caring, his sense of humor, and with his generous nature— many of the qualities her brothers had.

Within seven days of their arranged meeting, Benazir agreed to become engaged to Asif Ali Zardari. In December 1987, the Bhutto-Zardari wedding took place before two hundred guests at 70 Clifton. A ceremony was also held before thousands at the Lyari stadium, where the crowds cheered for the newly married couple.

A number of Muslim customs were bypassed for their marriage. The rule requiring two weeks of isolation for a bride-to-be was ignored because of Bhutto's work schedule. Also, instead of the seven sets of jewelry traditionally given to the bride

from the groom, she preferred to receive two simple sets. She also decided to keep her father's name instead of taking her husband's.

The marriage conditions, traditionally chanted by family and friends, were vastly different from the typical vows. Asif had to agree to look after any children, and to allow his wife to go to jail for the sake of her beliefs. "You must agree that Benazir will serve the nation," the Bhutto family sang.

"That is all right with me, for I will serve the nation by serving my wife," Asif replied.

At the age of thirty-four, Benazir had entered a warm and understanding marriage that the Muslim world could approve of. But contrary to what Zia's government thought, she was not giving up politics. She promised to continue her political fight against Zia's government.

At the end of May 1988, Zia made a surprise move. He dissolved Parliament and called for free elections in ninety days. The members of the PPP were overjoyed, but Bhutto was suspicious. This had happened too many times before. She thought there must be some political reason for him to make such a move.

Sanam offered a possible reason for Zia's action. Zia's announcement followed another announcement made by Benazir and Asif: they were

Asif Zardari and Benazir Bhutto on their wedding day.

expecting their first child in September. Sanam
guessed that Zia expected Bhutto to stay at home
and not campaign. He might have also believed
that her recent marriage and new baby would turn
voters against her.

In preparing for the upcoming elections, Zia
passed even stricter laws. The first was to declare
Shariah, or Islamic law, as the supreme law of the
land. According to Shariah, an ordinary citizen
could take any law to the high courts and call it
un-Islamic. In this way, Zia hoped someone would
challenge the right of women to run for high government offices. This could make it unlawful for
Bhutto to be a leading candidate. However, the con-
titution of 1973 made it legal for women to enter
elections, so Zia's plan failed.

Zia's next action was to make all nine political
parties register with the government. This would
give him the power to decide which parties could
participate in the elections. Fortunately, the PPP
presented a strong case before the Supreme Court
against the government and won. The court agreed
that Zia's action was illegal according to the constitution.

An unexpected accident in the summer of 1988
changed the course of events for Pakistan and for
Bhutto. On August 17, Bhutto learned that General

Zia's plane had crashed after take-off in a Punjabi town. All thirty passengers were said to be dead, including General Zia and the United States ambassador to Pakistan.

Bhutto was stunned by the thought that eleven years of dictatorship might finally be over. She could not be completely happy, though. She knew that martial law could be declared. To her relief, Pakistan's former chairman of the senate took over as president, and announced that the elections would be held as scheduled.

The shocking news of Zia's death led to many rumors. Some viewed the crash as an act of God, while others thought someone might have tampered with the aircraft. Still others believed that India had fired a missile and downed the plane, or that the Soviet's had sought revenge for Zia's support of the Afghan rebels. Although the facts were never fully uncovered, most experts agreed it was a mechanical failure in the plane.

Although Zia was no longer a threat to her, Bhutto continued to campaign. Nearly 18,000 candidates had registered for 700 national and provincial government seats. With 80 percent of the population expected to vote, Bhutto could not afford to waste time.

Her activities were interrupted on September

21, 1988, when her son Bilawal, meaning, "one without equal," was born. From the beginning, Asif treasured his son, saying "He looks just like me." Benazir was happy that her son would have the same father's love she had felt from Ali Bhutto.

Within five days of Bilawal's birth, Bhutto was back at work. Zia's death had not stopped the threats and violence aimed at Bhutto and the PPP. But wherever she went, large, enthusiastic crowds greeted her.

When the polls were closed on November 16, 1988, the PPP had won major political contests in all four provinces, including 92 seats in the National Assembly. On December 1, Benazir Bhutto was declared prime minister of Pakistan. Not only was she the first woman to lead a Muslim nation, but at thirty-five years of age, she was one of the youngest heads of state in the world.

In the forty-one years since Pakistan's creation, there had only been one democratic, free election—her father's in 1977. Now, for the second time in history, a Bhutto was attempting to bring democracy to Pakistan.

Chapter/Ten

Making Democracy Work

Following the election, the streets of Pakistan were filled with people celebrating their new leader. Posters and cardboard cut-outs of her appeared on walls or in the middle of traffic circles. Every major city in Pakistan was ablaze with color and a carnival-like atmosphere.

Bhutto had little time to celebrate. She began the huge task of restoring democracy to her nation and healing the wounds of dictatorship. She and her family moved from Asif's house in Karachi to the capital, Islamabad.

The new prime minister was faced with many problems. Dealing with the military was one of her most difficult tasks. Military leaders had been in power for most of Pakistan's four decades,

especially during Zia's eleven-year reign. Throughout this period, the armed forces had become more
and more corrupt, or dishonest. Some sources
claimed this was caused by low wages. If people
offered the soldiers money for favors, many of
them accepted. This resulted in widespread bribery.

From the time Bhutto became prime minister,
the military kept a careful watch on her policies.
They were concerned about whether or not she
would cut their budget. According to Pakistani
newspapers, military officials were also waiting to
see whether a civilian government could maintain
law and order without them.

Pakistan's relationship with Afghanistan was
another difficult issue for Bhutto. While the Soviets still occupied Afghanistan, Pakistan would not
recognize the Afghan government. Once the Soviet
army left in 1988, however, this policy had to
change. During the ten-year Soviet occupation, an
unofficial government made up of Afghan refugees
had been formed in Peshawar, Pakistan, near the
border with Afghanistan. Pakistan, under Zia's
rule, had recognized this group as the real, democratic government of Afghanistan.

Yet when the Soviets pulled out of Afghanistan
in 1988, they left behind their own appointed
leaders. In order to keep peace, Bhutto now had to

deal with both the existing government in Kabul,
the capital of Afghanistan, and the unofficial one
in Peshawar. Until Afghanistan holds free elections, Bhutto's dealings with that country require
great patience and diplomacy.

As a result of the Afghan war, drug trafficking
in Pakistan has increased. Since the beginning of
the war, an estimated 700,000 Pakistanis have
become heroin addicts. To fight this problem,
Bhutto has encouraged the growers of poppy
seeds—which are used in making heroin—to plow
up their fields and plant orchards and onions instead. These bring as much profit as the poppies.

Many observers think that Bhutto may be able
to resolve the problems with Afghanistan and
drugs. Pakistan's relationship with India, though,
continues to be a difficult issue.

After she took office, Bhutto and India's
Prime Minister Rajiv Gandhi tried to solve the
problems between Pakistan and India. In addition
to some cultural exchanges, both leaders had
agreed not to use nuclear force against each
other. Since the two countries have always been
rivals, Bhutto was criticized for making these
agreements. Many critics said that she had given in
to India. Gandhi was defeated in 1989, however.
With that country's new leadership, the future

relationship between the two neighbors remains
uncertain.

Since her election, Bhutto has tried to reform
the education system. At the present time, nearly
74 percent of Pakistanis cannot read or write. Bhutto hopes to change this. With her new minister of
state for education, Shahnaz Wazir Ali, Bhutto is
trying to offer more Pakistanis an education.

There is some resistance to these efforts, however, among Muslim men and religious leaders
who do not want girls or women to go to school.
Also, rural families often need their oldest children
to stay home and look after the younger ones, or
to work to help support the family.

Bhutto has had more success in helping older
children. She has started a technical training pro-
gram for young people who are educated, but cannot find jobs. Critics, however, say she should
have done this much sooner after her election.

In order to provide more jobs for all Pakistanis, Bhutto has been working to improve the
country's economy. New plans to develop Pakistan's manufacturing and agricultural industries
have been designed. Also, to encourage investment
in the country, Bhutto wants to make it easier for
new private companies to get started. She has rec-
ommended lowering taxes for them and decreasing

the time it takes to get permits.

Pakistan has just re-entered the British Commonwealth, an organization of nations who have promised to cooperate with Great Britain. This gives it many opportunities to increase its fortunes by lowering the cost of trading with Great Britain and other European countries. Also, in May 1990, the country will experiment with privatization—allowing publicly owned companies to become privately owned.

The pressures on Benazir Bhutto as prime minister, and as a young woman with a growing family, are enormous. As a result, the time she spends with her family is valued. When she travels to other countries for conferences and metings, Asif and Bilawal often go with her. Sometimes, Bilawal rides with her to work in the mornings. He might also be there to greet her at the end of the day. Since she is gone for most of the day, this is a private time when they can be together.

Bhutto's work day is a long one. She usually reaches her office at the General Secretariat at 8:00 A.M. each morning. The office is large and square, paneled in wood and carpeted in soft gray with matching gray curtains. Two sofas face each other, separated by a long table filled with magazines, newspapers, and an appointment book. The Paki-

The prime minister and her son, Bilawal, share a quiet moment together.

stani and PPP flags hang behind her desk of simply carved, dark wood. Chests stand against the walls, and the only personal touch is a crystal vase filled with fresh flowers.

Bhutto's clothes are made up of a variety of shalwar kamiz in bright colors. Her dupatta is usually white, but, on occasion, she wears a yellow one. Tall and slender, Bhutto's skin is fair and her eyes a deep brown. She looks directly at the person with whom she is talking, and offers a firm handshake.

As soon as Bhutto arrives each day, her military secretary hands her a schedule of appointments. Throughout the day, two male attendants stand on either side of her office door. They wear tan shalwar kamiz with bright red vests and hats. The attendants serve the visitors and act as messengers and guards. Although Bhutto's appointments finish at 5:00 P.M., the receptions, policy meetings, and visiting diplomats and heads of state usually extend her day to fourteen and sometimes sixteen hours.

"I used to spend sixteen hours a day in a jeep with the heat beating down on me," Bhutto recalls. "We would sleep for a few hours and get up again. I was never tired. Now I work from eight to five, and I go home tired."

After a long day, Bhutto returns to the prime minister's residence, high on a sloping hill, ten minutes away from her office. The house, with a grand view of Islamabad, once belonged to the chief minister of Sindh. Bhutto felt it suited the needs of her family better than the official residence in Rawalpindi.

In addition to the many duties she has in Pakistan, Bhutto frequently visits other countries to deliver speeches. In June 1989, she was invited to the United States to speak before a joint session of Congress. In her Pakistani national dress and white chiffon scarf, her words about Pakistan's newfound freedom filled the chamber. The members applauded this new leader of Pakistan.

"My friends, freedom is not an end," Bhutto declared. "Freedom is a beginning. Let us stand together now as the people of Pakistan strive to give meaning to their newfound freedom. Come with us toward a tomorrow better than all the yesterdays we knew. History, the rush of events, perhaps even destiny, has brought me here today...."

As the members listened attentively, Bhutto continued. "As a representative of the young, let me be viewed as one of the new generation of leaders, unshackled by the constraints and irrational hatreds of the past. As a representative of women, let my message be, 'Yes, you can.' And as a believer in Islam...let my message be about a compassionate and tolerant religion, teaching hard work and family values under a merciful God."

After her appearance before Congress, Benazir and Asif were honored at a White House dinner. During her visit, President George Bush promised to give $4.2 billion in financial aid to Pakistan over the course of six years. Bush also said the United States would supply Pakistan with 60 fighter

Prime Minister Bhutto met with President George Bush in 1989 to discuss financial aid to Pakistan.

bombers and an additional $600 million for economic and military aid. In return, Bhutto had to promise she would not let her country become a nuclear power.

Early in 1990, however, Bhutto made an agreement with China in which that country agreed to build a nuclear power station for Pakistan. Although Bhutto denied any intentions of using the power for defensive weapons, doubts have been expressed by India and other countries.

While still in Washington, D.C., in 1989, Benazir Bhutto met with fifteen of her friends from Harvard. According to her Harvard roommate, Yolanda Kodrzycki Henderson, "The meeting at Blair House was special. We talked as friends. She had a sense of what the ordinary people of Pakistan want. Despite her wealth, I've seen her among rural people, and she knows and understands what their aspirations [hopes] are....She is very adaptable, as she was at Radcliffe when she first arrived at the age of sixteen."

From the nation's capital, Prime Minister Bhutto traveled to Cambridge, Massachusetts. There, she gave the commencement address at Harvard University to the 1989 graduating class. For her, it was a sentimental time. In the soft rain, she spoke mainly about freedom and democracy, and how Pakistan had fought for it.

In a 1989 interview, Bhutto was asked for her advice to young people, and to her own children. The prime minister said she hoped they would "learn to stand on their own two feet...to have confidence in themselves...and to be patient. People ruin their chances by impatience and by wanting too much too soon. I would want them to be a good sport and know that they will win some and lose some."

Bhutto returned to Harvard University in 1989 to address the graduating seniors.

When Bhutto returned from the United States after her visit, she continued to face growing opposition. Her critics accused her of not making changes fast enough. Others said she was using the Bhutto name to get what she wanted. They also accused Asif of making business deals for the government and taking 10 percent of each deal. Angered, Bhutto defended her husband and demanded evidence to back up these accusations.

One of the prime minister's closest and most respected associates has said, "It is very difficult for her to get things done because she has to pay attention to the political parties and pressures that would try to unseat her....She does not know whom to trust—even those closest to her. She is very bright—far more intelligent than any around her. I would not like to confront the problems facing her, such as a 3 percent population increase annually, but she has patience."

One of the most frustrating problems facing Bhutto now is the issue of women's rights. For years, Pakistani women have had far fewer rights than women in many other nations. One of Bhutto's goals is to achieve equal rights for Pakistani women. Her chief political rivals, however, as well as many Pakistani men, are against any change in current laws. These opponents criticize her of wanting to make too many changes. Others accuse her of moving too slowly.

Fortunately, Bhutto has learned how to deal with criticism by the press and by her government. "To cope with criticism," she said, "I don't start my day by reading newspapers. My press secretary presents me with a written summary. I get through what I have to do. By evening, I'm thick-skinned. Actually, I don't mind criticism. I know I'm not an angel. The press is a fact of life."

In November 1989, the criticism against Bhutto reached a high point. The National Assembly decided to take a vote of "no confidence" against the prime minister and the PPP. If a majority of National Assembly members had voted against her, a new national election would have been called. But Bhutto and the PPP survived this election by twelve votes and remained in power.

After the election, Bhutto's cabinet resigned, allowing her to select new members. Some came from political parties other than the PPP. Advisers felt this would help to increase her popularity.

The move from critic to leader has not been easy for Bhutto. Her main political rival is Nawaz Sharif, the chief minister of Punjab province. He has criticized the prime minister for failing to be an effective leader, wasting opportunities, and for not passing any major new laws. Bhutto also faces opposition from President Ghulam Ishaq Khan. They have not had a good relationship, due in part to the president's former association with General Zia.

In spite of these political troubles, Benazir Bhutto is greatly admired by most Pakistanis and by many world leaders. Before Benazir had completed her first year in office, Nusrat Bhutto—now

Benazir's senior minister—traveled to the United States. There, she accepted the Averrell W. Harriman Award for her daughter's role in restoring democracy to Pakistan.

"The principle of humanity should be promoted, and we should reach out to each other because we are all the creatures of God," Benazir Bhutto has said. She tries to promote the principles of humanity—being respectful to each other— in her own life. Although she was imprisoned by her opponents for nearly ten years, she holds no bitterness toward them.

"The last words my father said to me from his jail in Rawalpindi were, 'I don't want you to be bitter.' Every time I would feel bitter, I would think of this. I didn't want to fail him." Benazir hopes to pass on these beliefs to her son, Bilawal, and to her daughter, Bakhatawar, who was born January 25, 1990. In the Sindhi language, Bakhatawar means "full of hope."

To the world, Benazir Bhutto has become a symbol of freedom. To Pakistanis, she has become a hope for a better future. The prime minister has her own vision for Pakistan: "I would like Pakistan to be at peace with its neighbors. I would like it to be stable and independent. I would like Pakistan to emerge out of the darkness of illiteracy and have the world judge our country on its talents and merits. I would like to see equal opportunities for men and women, and have other Asian countries point to Pakistan and say, 'If Pakistan can break through illiteracy, so can we.' "

It is too early to tell if Bhutto's vision for the struggling nation of Pakistan will be achieved. Yet, whether or not she reaches her goals, her belief in her abilities, and in the future of her country, will not falter. "When you believe," the young prime minister states, "then there is no mountain high enough to scale. That is my message to the youth of America, to its women, and to its people."

Afterword

It has been fifteen months since that momentous day, December 2, 1988, when I took the oath of office to become prime minister of the Islamic Republic of Pakistan. For my country, my people, and for me, these months have been a time of great change and challenge. Eleven years of military dictatorship had devastated the economy and the social fabric of Pakistan....worst of all, an entire generation of young Pakistanis has grown up without knowledge of their responsibilities and rights under democracy.

We are determined to build a new Pakistan, a democratic Pakistan, committed to equality under the law for all people, for men and women alike. We want a Pakistan which fulfills the basic social and economic needs of a people...a Pakistan committed to...bring our nation into the twenty-first century. This we owe to our children...and to them, we dedicate our administration. Pakistan is a land of great promise, and we hope our friends everywhere will help us as we endeavor to build a new nation.

— *Benazir Bhutto*

Selected Bibliography

Books

Bhutto, Benazir. *Daughter of Destiny*. New York: Simon and Schuster, 1989.

Pakistan. Ministry of Information and Broadcasting. *Facts about Pakistan*. Directorate of Films and Publications. 1988.

_____. *Speeches and Statements of Benazir Bhutto, December 2, 1988, to April 30, 1989*. Directorate of Films and Publications. 1989.

_____. *Visit to the United States of America, June 5-11, 1989*. Directorate of Films and Publications. 1989.

Newspapers and Journals

"Benazir Comes in off the Streets." *The Economist* (November 21, 1987): 48.

"Bhutto Gets Tough." *Time* (June 5, 1989): 33.

Christian Science Monitor. March 14, 1989.

Dawn. Karachi, Pakistan. September 25-October 1, 1989.

Fadiman, Anne. "Behind the Veil." *Life* (January 1987): 19.

_____. "Benazir: Face to Face with the Woman Who Wants to Rule Pakistan." *Life* (October 1989): 51-58.

Galbraith, Peter. "The Return of Benazir Bhutto." *Harvard* Magazine (July/August 1989): 19.

Henderson, Yolanda. "My Roommate, the Future Prime Minister." *Radcliffe Quarterly* (June 1989): 18.

Los Angeles Times. June 8, 1989.

New York Times. June 9, 1989. November 1, 1989.

"Now the Hard Part. Governing." *Time* (December 12, 1988): 47.

Pakistani Times. October 1-7, 1989.

Starr, Kevin. "At Harvard, She was Called Pinkie." *Vogue* (April 1989): 416.

Interviews

Bhutto, Benazir. Interview with the author. Islamabad, Pakistan. October 5, 1989.

Fadiman, Anne. Telephone interview with author. August 4, 1989.

Galbraith, Peter. Telephone interview with author. September 6, 1989.

Henderson, Yolanda Kodrzycki. Telephone interview with author. August 15, 1989.

Waheed, Samiya. Interview with author. Islamabad, Pakistan. October 5, 1989.

Index

ADDENDUM

Since the publication of this book, Benazir Bhutto
was expelled from office in August 1990 by the president.
She was accused of being incompetent and her husband
of taking bribes allegedly for business deals made with
other countries. He was jailed for two years.

Once again, the president dismissed the Nawaz Sharif
government in July 1993. Benazir's Pakistan Peoples
Party won the elections, and she returned to the post of
prime minister.

Her political misfortunes surfaced again in 1996 when
the President removed Benazir from office. Despite her
protests, allegations of corruption and misrule plagued her
government. Also, her husband was accused of hiding
millions of dollars in Swiss banks.

In addition, Benazir's husband was accused of
arranging the murder of her brother, Murataza Bhutto,
who wanted to become prime minister and replace his
sister. Benazir's mother wanted her son to be prime
minister rather than her daughter.

The sentence for charges against her was a five year
prison term and an $8.6 million fine. She and her husband
were cleared by courts of law in Switzerland and Canada.

When the millenium began, Benazir and her three
children remained in exile in London when a military
government assumed power. Benazir's husband has been
imprisoned in Pakistan since 1996.

About the Author

Libby Hughes is an author playwright. Her published biographies include Margaret Thatcher, Nelson Mandela, Colin Powell, Norman Schwarzkopf, Benazir Bhutto, Christopher Reeve, and Tiger Woods. Hughes edited Ginger Rogers' autobiography and is listed in the Who's Who of American Women. Her plays have won contests and been produced off off Broadway. She lives in Cape Cod.

AUTHORS GUILD BACKINPRINT.COM EDITIONS are fiction and nonfiction works that were originally brought to the reading public by established United States publishers but have fallen out of print. The economics of traditional publishing methods force tens of thousands of works out of print each year, eventually claiming many, if not most, award-winning and one-time best-selling titles. With improvements in print-on-demand technology, authors and their estates, in cooperation with the Authors Guild, are making some of these works available again to readers in quality paperback editions. Authors Guild Backinprint.com Editions may be found at nearly all online bookstores and are also available from traditional booksellers. For further information or to purchase any Backinprint.com title please visit www.backinprint.com.

Except as noted on their copyright pages, Authors Guild Backinprint.com Editions are presented in their original form. Some authors have chosen to revise or update their works with new information. The Authors Guild is not the editor or publisher of these works and is not responsible for any of the content of these editions.

THE AUTHORS GUILD is the nation's largest society of published book authors. Since 1912 it has been the leading writers' advocate for fair compensation, effective copyright protection, and free expression. Further information is available at www.authorsguild.org.

Please direct inquiries about the Authors Guild and Backinprint.com Editions to the Authors Guild offices in New York City, or e-mail staff@backinprint.com.

0-595-00388-5

Printed in the United States
99133LV00001B/215/A